☐ N~7
r

D0730397

# GARDEN
# BIRDS

J 598.8 LIN
Lindsey, Terrence
Garden birds

WITHDRAWN

062705

FJUL 2 9 2005

**ROCKFORD PUBLIC LIBRARY**
Rockford, Illinois
www.rockfordpubliclibrary.org
815-965-9511

Text: Helen Cooney
Illustrations: Dr. David S. Kirshner
Consultant: Terence Lindsey

Copyright © 1996 by the National Geographic Society

First Trade Edition 2001

**Published by**
The National Geographic Society
John M. Fahey, Jr., President and Chief Executive Officer
Gilbert M. Grosvenor, Chairman of the Board
Nina D. Hoffman, Executive Vice President,
President of Books and School Publishing
William R. Gray, Vice President and Director, Book Division
Nancy Laties Feresten, Director of Children's Publishing
Barbara Brownell, Director of Continuities
Mark A. Caraluzzi, Vice President, Sales and Marketing
Vincent P. Ryan, Manufacturing Manager

All rights reserved. No part of this book may be reproduced or transmitted
in any form or by any means, electronic or mechanical, including photocopying,
without permission in writing from the National Geographic Society/
1145 17th Street N.W./Washington, D.C. 20036–4688.

Library of Congress Catalog Number: 96-068038

ISBN: 0-7922-3420-0

Trade Edition ISBN: 0-7922-6572-6

Produced for the National Geographic Society by Weldon Owen Pty Ltd
43 Victoria Street, McMahons Point, NSW 2060, Australia
A member of the Weldon Owen Group of Companies
Sydney • San Francisco • London

Chairman: Kevin Weldon
President: John Owen
Publisher: Sheena Coupe
Managing Editor: Ariana Klepac
Art Director: Sue Burk
Senior Designer: Mark Thacker
Designer: Regina Safro
Text Editors: Robert Coupe, Paulette Kay
Photo Researcher: Elizabeth Connolly
Production Director: Mick Bagnato
Production Manager: Simone Perryman

Film production by Mandarin Offset
Printed in Mexico

# NATIONAL GEOGRAPHIC

## my first pocket Guide

# GARDEN BIRDS

TERENCE LINDSEY

ROCKFORD PUBLIC LIBRARY

# INTRODUCTION

**B**irds come in many shapes and sizes—from tiny, hovering hummingbirds to tall ostriches that run instead of fly. The one thing that makes a bird different from any other animal is that it has feathers. Birds have bony backbones, they breathe air through lungs, and they lay eggs that have hard shells. They also care for their young until they are strong enough to leave the nest.

Whether you live in a bustling city or in the wide-open spaces, you are likely to see some of the birds in this book. Some birds are seen all year round, while others appear only during the summer or winter. There are some kinds that live right across North America, and others that live only in one area.

Many small birds visit gardens, especially if you have seeds or fruit for them to eat. Make sure you keep feeding them right throughout the winter—otherwise they may not be able to find enough food to eat in the wild. Try not to disturb birds' nests or eggs because parent birds may stay away if humans are around.

## HOW TO USE THIS BOOK

Each spread in this book helps you to identify one kind of bird. It gives you information about the bird's size, color, appearance, and behavior. You can see how long it is by using the ruler on the inside of the back cover. "Where To Find" has a map of North America that is shaded to show you where the bird lives. Discover an unusual fact about the bird in the "Field Note," and see it in its natural environment in the photograph. If you find a word you do not know, look it up in the Glossary on page 76.

# RUBY-THROATED HUMMINGBIRD

 Ruby-throated hummingbirds have long, needle-like bills. When they fly, their wings beat so fast that they make a humming sound. Only the males have ruby-red throats.

## WHERE TO FIND:

You can often see these birds in parks and gardens in most parts of eastern North America.

## WHAT TO LOOK FOR:

* **SIZE**

Ruby-throated hummingbirds are about as long as a baseball card.

* **COLOR**

Their backs and heads are shimmering green. Underneath they are dull white.

* **OTHER FEATURES**

Hummingbirds make short, squeaky noises. They do not sing.

* **BEHAVIOR**

They stick their bills into flowers to lick up the nectar with their long tongues.

A hummingbird's wings beat 75 times a second—so fast that you see only a blur.

FIELD NOTES
Hummingbirds are the only birds that can hover in one spot, and that can fly backward.

# DOWNY WOODPECKER

 Downy woodpeckers are common in most parts of North America. In cities and towns you might hear the sound of their short, stubby bills drumming on telephone poles.

## WHERE TO FIND:
You usually see downy woodpeckers perching on trees in parks, forests, orchards, and woods.

## WHAT TO LOOK FOR:

✳ **SIZE**
Downy woodpeckers are about as long as this book.

✳ **COLOR**
They have plain white backs and black wings with white bars and spots.

✳ **OTHER FEATURES**
The downy woodpecker's song sounds like a horse's whinny.

✳ **BEHAVIOR**
They use their bills to dig into the bark of trees and find spiders and insects.

The male downy woodpecker has a red patch on the back of its crown. The female has a white patch.

## FIELD NOTES

Downy woodpeckers have stiff, pointed tail feathers that support the birds as they cling to tree trunks.

# SCISSOR-TAILED FLYCATCHER

 The scissor-tailed flycatcher is the state bird of Oklahoma. Its scissor-like tail is easy to recognize as the bird swoops gracefully from telephone wires to catch flying insects.

## WHERE TO FIND:
These birds live mainly in grasslands. They often sit on roadside fence posts and dead trees.

## WHAT TO LOOK FOR:

**✳ SIZE**
Male scissor-tailed flycatchers are about 14 inches long, including their tails. Females have slightly shorter tails.

**✳ COLOR**
They are pale gray, with soft, salmon-pink on the sides.

**✳ OTHER FEATURES**
They have long, forked tails.

**✳ BEHAVIOR**
These noisy birds often chase other birds much larger than themselves.

This bird gets its name from its long tail that looks like the blades of a pair of scissors.

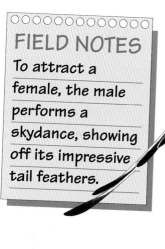

## FIELD NOTES

To attract a female, the male performs a skydance, showing off its impressive tail feathers.

# BARN SWALLOW

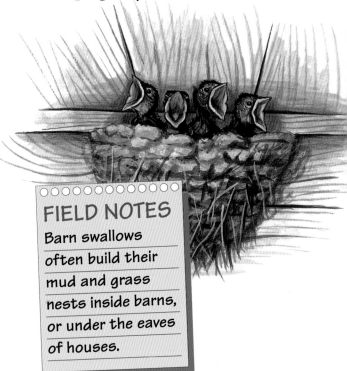

Barn swallows dart low above fields and lawns to catch insects in their short, wide bills. They can even drink as they fly, dipping down over rivers and lakes to scoop up tiny mouthfuls.

## FIELD NOTES

Barn swallows often build their mud and grass nests inside barns, or under the eaves of houses.

The barn swallow has a narrow, dark band across its breast.

## WHERE TO FIND:
Barn swallows live in open country, but you can often see them around buildings or in city parks.

## WHAT TO LOOK FOR:

✳ **SIZE**
These sleek birds are seven inches long—about as long as an average pencil.

✳ **COLOR**
They are glossy blue on the back, reddish underneath, and rust-colored on the throat.

✳ **OTHER FEATURES**
They have forked tails with white spots.

✳ **BEHAVIOR**
These birds migrate to Central or South America for the winter.

13

# BLUE JAY

 The blue jay is one of the boldest and showiest birds around. It swoops and glides through the forest, sounding a noisy alarm if it senses that danger is close by.

## WHERE TO FIND:

Blue jays live in forests, wooded lots, swamps, farmlands, parks, and the backyards of houses.

## WHAT TO LOOK FOR:

**✳ SIZE**
Blue jays are about one foot long.

**✳ COLOR**
The blue jay is blue and white on the back, and pale gray underneath.

**✳ OTHER FEATURES**
It has a crest of blue feathers on its head. It can raise and lower this crest.

**✳ BEHAVIOR**
It often scares small birds from their nests by screaming like a hawk. Then it eats their eggs.

The blue jay has a band of black around its throat.

Blue jays often forget where they buried acorns to eat in winter. Later, oak trees sprout from the nuts.

15

# AMERICAN CROW

 A big black crow flying slowly overhead is a familiar sight across North America. When the trees are bare during the winter, you can often see the crows' bulky stick nests high in the treetops.

## WHERE TO FIND:
You may see crows almost anywhere, but they usually live in open country and around farms.

## WHAT TO LOOK FOR:

**✳ SIZE**
Crows are about 19 inches long.

**✳ COLOR**
Crows are entirely black, including their bills and feet.

**✳ OTHER FEATURES**
The most common call of the crow is a harsh *caw*.

**✳ BEHAVIOR**
Crows often chase hawks and owls, but they will fly away if humans come too close.

The American crow usually feeds on the ground.

FIELD NOTES

Crows gather in flocks. One or two stand guard while the others search for fruit, nuts, insects, and mice.

# BLACK-CAPPED CHICKADEE

 The black-capped chickadee is the state bird of Maine and Massachusetts. It is an acrobatic bird that twists and turns upside down while it feeds.

**WHERE TO FIND:**
Black-capped chickadees live in woodlands. They also perch in trees in gardens and parks.

## WHAT TO LOOK FOR:

**✴ SIZE**
Black-capped chickadees are slightly longer than five inches.

**✴ COLOR**
They are gray on the back and white underneath, with white cheeks, and black caps and bibs.

**✴ OTHER FEATURES**
They have a *chick-a-dee-dee-dee* call.

**✴ BEHAVIOR**
They eat insects and spiders in summer, and berries and seeds in winter.

The black-capped chickadee is a small, plump bird with a tiny bill.

FIELD NOTES

The chickadee is so tame it will take a peanut from your hand—particularly in winter, when food is scarce.

# BUSHTIT

 The bushtit is rarely seen alone. Up to 20 of these active birds will suddenly appear in the bushes, twittering noisily. They eat small insects and spiders, as well as berries and seeds.

## WHERE TO FIND:
Bushtits gather on the smaller branches of trees in open country, parks, and gardens.

## WHAT TO LOOK FOR:

✳ **SIZE**
Bushtits are just over four inches long.

✳ **COLOR**
They are dark gray above and lighter gray underneath.

✳ **OTHER FEATURES**
Their nests, which look like small pouches, are made of twigs, grasses, and moss, held together with spider web.

✳ **BEHAVIOR**
Bushtits sometimes hang upside down when they are feeding.

The bushtit is a fluffy little bird with a long tail and a short, pointed bill.

**FIELD NOTES**

Bushtits are hardly ever still. They fly in flocks, following each other constantly from bush to bush.

# WHITE-BREASTED NUTHATCH

White-breasted nuthatches run down tree trunks, clinging with their strong feet and sharp claws. They forage under the bark with their long, pointed bills for insects.

## WHERE TO FIND:

They perch on tree trunks and branches in woodlands, and in parks, orchards, and gardens.

## WHAT TO LOOK FOR:

* **SIZE**
A white-breasted nuthatch is almost as long as this book.

* **COLOR**
It is blue-gray on the back and white underneath. The male has a black cap on its head. The female's cap is gray.

* **OTHER FEATURES**
Its call sounds like *yank, yank, yank*.

* **BEHAVIOR**
White-breasted nuthatches live together in pairs all year round.

White-breasted nuthatches often store the seeds they collect from bird feeders in their nests.

FIELD NOTES

The white-breasted nuthatch can walk head first down a tree trunk or even a dangling clothesline.

23

# CAROLINA WREN

The Carolina wren is the state bird of South Carolina. It is sometimes hard to see because it lives in thick, tangled bushes. It makes loud, chattering noises if intruders come too close.

## WHERE TO FIND:
Carolina wrens hop around in gardens and parks, usually out of sight in the undergrowth.

## WHAT TO LOOK FOR:

**✳ SIZE**
The Carolina wren is six inches long.

**✳ COLOR**
It is rusty brown on the back and pale cinnamon underneath. It has a large, white stripe over each eye.

**✳ OTHER FEATURES**
It makes a nest in a tree trunk, using twigs, grasses, and leaves.

**✳ BEHAVIOR**
The Carolina wren eats insects in summer, and berries and seeds in winter.

The Carolina wren is a shy bird, but if you make a squeaking noise, you might tempt one out of its hiding place.

## FIELD NOTES

The Carolina wren's familiar *tea-kettle, tea-kettle* song is heard all year round, especially on warm days.

# AMERICAN DIPPER

American dippers fly swiftly over bubbling streams, then dive suddenly into the water—right down to the bottom. There they eat their fill of insects. They bob up to the surface to take breaths.

**WHERE TO FIND:**
American dippers usually live in pairs, near streams, in the high mountain areas of western North America.

**WHAT TO LOOK FOR:**

✳ **SIZE**
Dippers are about eight inches long. They are plump with stubby tails.

✳ **COLOR**
Except for white eyelids, they are plain, smoky gray.

✳ **OTHER FEATURES**
When it sings, the dipper makes a loud, clear, warbling sound.

✳ **BEHAVIOR**
Dippers bob up and down as they perch on streamside boulders.

The American dipper
is the only songbird
that feeds underwater.

**FIELD NOTES**

American dippers
have strong feet
that help them
cling to slippery
rocks in rushing
streams.

# RUBY-CROWNED KINGLET

 Ruby-crowned kinglets often feed in flocks with other small birds. They flit around branches, picking off insects and seeds. Sometimes they look for food on the ground.

## WHERE TO FIND:
Ruby-crowned kinglets spend summer in pine forests. In winter, you may see them in parks and thickets.

## WHAT TO LOOK FOR:

**✳ SIZE**
The ruby-crowned kinglet is just over four inches long.

**✳ COLOR**
It is dull green on the back and pale underneath. Its wings have white bars.

**✳ OTHER FEATURES**
It has a pale ring around each eye, and a slender bill.

**✳ BEHAVIOR**
It flicks its wings in and out as it hovers near branches in search of food.

From bill tip to tail tip, this tiny, active bird is much smaller than a canary.

FIELD NOTES

The male kinglet has a red patch hidden under its head feathers. It reveals this patch when it is excited.

# MOUNTAIN BLUEBIRD

 The mountain bluebird is the state bird of Idaho and Nevada. This tame bird is often seen around ranch houses. It has brilliant blue plumage.

**WHERE TO FIND:**
Look for mountain bluebirds in farmyards, desert regions, and other areas with few trees.

## WHAT TO LOOK FOR:

**✳ SIZE**
Adult mountain bluebirds are just over seven inches long.

**✳ COLOR**
Males have sky-blue backs and paler blue underparts. Females are gray with some blue on their wings and tails.

**✳ OTHER FEATURES**
These birds usually live in pairs.

**✳ BEHAVIOR**
Mountain bluebirds rarely sing. If they do, it is usually just before sunrise.

Mountain bluebirds pounce on insects from low tree branches.

FIELD NOTES
These birds often nest in snug tree hollows. As trees are cut down, many bluebirds lose their homes.

# HERMIT THRUSH

 The hermit thrush is the state bird of Vermont. It spends most of its time in forest shrubs and undergrowth. Every year, hermit thrushes nest in northern forests. They fly south to Mexico for the winter.

## WHERE TO FIND:
Hermit thrushes live in forests. In summer, look for them in woods, thickets, and parks.

## WHAT TO LOOK FOR:

**✳ SIZE**
A hermit thrush is seven inches long—about the length of an average pencil.

**✳ COLOR**
It is olive brown on the back and has a white breast with black spots.

**✳ OTHER FEATURES**
It feeds on the ground on insects, worms, snails, and berries.

**✳ BEHAVIOR**
It has a habit of raising its reddish tail, and then quickly flicking it down again.

The hermit thrush is often hard to see because it makes its home in the shady underbrush of the forest.

FIELD NOTES

The hermit thrush sings its haunting song to attract a mate and to scare off its rivals.

# AMERICAN ROBIN

 The American robin is the state bird of Connecticut, Michigan, and Wisconsin. When people hear the cheery song of this well-known bird, they know that spring is on the way.

## WHERE TO FIND:

American robins live in woods, gardens, and parks. You'll see them hopping about on your lawn.

## WHAT TO LOOK FOR:

✳ **SIZE**
The American robin is a medium-size bird. It is about ten inches long.

✳ **COLOR**
It has a dark gray back, a black head, and a reddish breast.

✳ **OTHER FEATURES**
It has a yellow bill and a white ring around each eye.

✳ **BEHAVIOR**
It makes a loud *chack-chack* sound before it roosts for the night.

In winter, when worms and snails are hard to find, the American robin eats berries.

**FIELD NOTES**

Robins cock their heads while they search for insects. They look as if they might be listening for worms.

# NORTHERN MOCKINGBIRD

 The northern mockingbird is the state bird of Arkansas, Florida, Mississippi, Tennessee, and Texas. Its rich and rambling song is often heard all night long.

## WHERE TO FIND:
Mockingbirds live in open country and farmlands. They are also common in parks and gardens.

## WHAT TO LOOK FOR:

**＊ SIZE**
An adult bird is just over ten inches long.

**＊ COLOR**
It has a pale gray back and is white underneath.

**＊ OTHER FEATURES**
It has white wing patches and white feathers on each side of its tail.

**＊ BEHAVIOR**
It flashes its white wing patches to scare off intruders.

The northern mockingbird can mimic other birds' calls and even a dog's bark.

**FIELD NOTES**

Northern mockingbirds often pick fights with other birds. They even chase crows and cats.

# BROWN THRASHER

 The brown thrasher is the state bird of Georgia. It spends most of its time creeping around in thick undergrowth, foraging for beetles and large insects. It has a long, melodious song.

## WHERE TO FIND:
Brown thrashers live among hedges and thick shrubs in forests, parks, and gardens.

## WHAT TO LOOK FOR:

**✳ SIZE**
A brown thrasher is just over 11 inches long.

**✳ COLOR**
It is red-brown on the back and white with brown streaks underneath.

**✳ OTHER FEATURES**
It has a long tail, a slightly curved bill, and yellow eyes.

**✳ BEHAVIOR**
It emerges from its usual dense cover, to sing out in the open.

The brown thrasher is about the same size and shape as a mockingbird.

## FIELD NOTES

The thrasher is a clever mimic. As well as singing its own song, it copies the songs of other birds.

# CEDAR WAXWING

 The cedar waxwing gets its name from the waxy red blobs on the tips of its wing feathers. Its favorite food is berries, particularly from the European mountain ash and the red cedar.

## WHERE TO FIND:
It lives in birch forests, woodlands, and orchards. It also visits berry trees in parks and gardens.

## WHAT TO LOOK FOR:

**✳ SIZE**
A cedar waxwing is just over seven inches long.

**✳ COLOR**
A cedar waxwing is mainly light brown. It has a gray rump.

**✳ OTHER FEATURES**
The cedar waxwing has a black face and a yellow-tipped tail.

**✳ BEHAVIOR**
Cedar waxwings usually fly in large flocks, hunting for food and eating.

Notice the cedar waxwing's crest above its black mask.

## FIELD NOTES

The cedar waxwing sometimes eats so many berries at one meal that it becomes too heavy to fly.

# LOGGERHEAD SHRIKE

 Loggerhead shrikes perch high up in dead trees, waiting to pounce on insects, mice, and small birds on the ground. Sometimes they chase small birds in flight.

## WHERE TO FIND:
Loggerhead shrikes live in open country and woodlands. They often sit alone on telephone wires.

## WHAT TO LOOK FOR:

✷ **SIZE**
A loggerhead shrike is about nine inches long.

✷ **COLOR**
It is soft gray on the back and white underneath. It has a black mask.

✷ **OTHER FEATURES**
It has black wings with white wing patches.

✷ **BEHAVIOR**
This bird is a skillful hunter. It also eats a lot of fruit.

You can recognize a loggerhead shrike
by its black mask and black wings
with white patches.

0000000000000

**FIELD NOTES**

A loggerhead
shrike often
stores its prey
on thorn spikes
until it is ready
to eat.

# EUROPEAN STARLING

In 1890, English settlers brought 68 European starlings to Central Park in New York. There are now over 200 million of these birds living across North America.

## FIELD NOTES

The European starling is one of the few birds that seems at home in the hustle and bustle of cities.

The European starling feeds on the ground, mainly on seeds and insects.

**WHERE TO FIND:**
Starlings live just about everywhere—from country roads to city streets.

## WHAT TO LOOK FOR:

**✴ SIZE**
Starlings are just over eight inches long.

**✴ COLOR**
They are glossy black, with a green and purple sheen. In winter and spring, their plumage has white speckles.

**✴ OTHER FEATURES**
In spring, starlings have yellow bills. Their bills turn dark gray in winter.

**✴ BEHAVIOR**
A starling's song is a jumble of squeaks, rattles, whistles, and chatters.

45

# RED-EYED VIREO

Red-eyed vireos (VI-ree-ohs) slowly move through tall trees in forests, picking off crawling insects. Their mellow, repetitive song echoes through the forest in the middle of the day.

## WHERE TO FIND:

Red-eyed vireos are hard to find because they live in the treetops of forests and woodlands.

## WHAT TO LOOK FOR:

**✳ SIZE**
A red-eyed vireo is almost as long as this book.

**✳ COLOR**
It is dull green on top and silky white underneath. It has a gray crown and white eyebrows.

**✳ OTHER FEATURES**
It has a thick bill with a tiny hook at the end.

**✳ BEHAVIOR**
It flies to South America for winter.

Only adult red-eyed vireos have red eyes. Young vireos have brownish eyes.

## FIELD NOTES

If a brown-headed cowbird lays its eggs in a vireo's nest, the vireo will tend the chicks when they hatch.

# YELLOW-RUMPED WARBLER

 The yellow-rumped warbler is an active little bird. You'll recognize it by the bright yellow patch on its rump. The male is more brightly colored than the female.

**WHERE TO FIND:**
In winter, you can see yellow-rumped warblers in gardens and fields. In summer, they live in cool pine forests.

## WHAT TO LOOK FOR:

**✳ SIZE**
The yellow-rumped warbler is just over five inches long.

**✳ COLOR**
The male is gray-blue and white with yellow sides. The female is brown and white. Both have yellow crowns.

**✳ OTHER FEATURES**
It eats insects, spiders, seeds, and berries.

**✳ BEHAVIOR**
Yellow-rumped warblers sometimes steal insects from spider webs.

Both the male and female yellow-rumped warbler have brown plumage in winter.

Western

Eastern

000000000000
FIELD NOTES
Western yellow-rumped warblers have yellow throats. Eastern birds have white throats.

# NORTHERN YELLOWTHROAT

In summer, the northern yellowthroat lives throughout North America, but it flies to South America for the winter. It feeds on small insects.

## FIELD NOTES

The northern yellowthroat takes shelter in bushes. It makes a scolding noise if an intruder comes near.

## WHERE TO FIND:
You may see northern yellowthroats in dense shrubs in damp, marshy areas, feeding on insects.

## WHAT TO LOOK FOR:

**✳ SIZE**
A northern yellowthroat is just over five inches long.

**✳ COLOR**
It has a dull green back and a bright yellow face and breast. The male has a black mask.

**✳ OTHER FEATURES**
It has a small bill and a short tail.

**✳ BEHAVIOR**
It sometimes comes out of the bushes if you make a *spish, spish* sound.

This male northern yellowthroat is in breeding plumage.

# NORTHERN CARDINAL

 Northern cardinals have loud, cheery whistles often heard on warm mornings. They forage for insects, berries, and seeds in the undergrowth of gardens and parks.

**WHERE TO FIND:**
Northern cardinals live in woodlands, swamplands, thickets, and hedges.

**WHAT TO LOOK FOR:**

✳ **SIZE**
Northern cardinals are about eight inches long.

✳ **COLOR**
Males are bright red with black faces and red bills. Females are grayish brown, with black faces.

✳ **OTHER FEATURES**
Both sexes have large crests.

✳ **BEHAVIOR**
Males and females sing all year round. Sometimes they sing together.

The northern cardinal is the state bird of Illinois, Indiana, Kentucky, North Carolina, Ohio, and West Virginia.

FIELD NOTES
The northern cardinal uses its short, deep, pointed bill like a nutcracker to crush seeds.

# CHESTNUT-SIDED TOWHEE

 Chestnut-sided towhees (TOE-heez) rarely leave the bushes and shrubs. Their song sounds like *drink-your-tea-ee-ee* and their call sounds like *toe-hee*.

**WHERE TO FIND:**
Chestnut-sided towhees live in the undergrowth of forests, parks, and gardens.

## WHAT TO LOOK FOR:

✳ **SIZE**
A chestnut-sided towhee is about eight inches long.

✳ **COLOR**
It is black on top, white underneath, and chestnut brown on the sides.

✳ **OTHER FEATURES**
It has white spots on the sides of its tail.

✳ **BEHAVIOR**
In the winter, it leaves Canada and the northern United States and flies farther south where it is warmer.

You will usually find a towhee on or near the ground, but not often out in the open like this one.

FIELD NOTES

If you hear a noisy scuffling sound, it could be a towhee searching through dead leaves for insects.

# LARK BUNTING

 The lark bunting is the state bird of Colorado. In fall and winter it often feeds by roadsides on insects and seeds. At breeding time, several pairs build their nests close together.

## WHERE TO FIND:
Look for lark buntings on the ground in prairies, plowed fields, and places with few trees.

## WHAT TO LOOK FOR:

**✳ SIZE**
Lark buntings are about seven inches long.

**✳ COLOR**
Males are black, with big white wing patches. Females have streaked brown and white coloring.

**✳ OTHER FEATURES**
Both males and females have streaked plumage in winter.

**✳ BEHAVIOR**
They often form large flocks in winter.

The lark bunting is small and stocky with a rounded tail and a thick, short bill.

## FIELD NOTES

Lark buntings sing while they fly. They rarely perch to sing because they live in places with few trees.

# SONG SPARROW

The song sparrow is one of the first birds to build its nest in spring. This is when you might hear its cheery, trilling song. It feeds on the ground on seeds, berries, and small insects.

Sparrow chick

## FIELD NOTES

Song sparrow chicks leave the nest when they are just ten days old—often before they can fly.

## WHERE TO FIND:
Song sparrows live near the ground, usually in damp areas. They often come into parks and gardens.

## WHAT TO LOOK FOR:

**✳ SIZE**
The song sparrow is just over six inches—about as long as this book.

**✳ COLOR**
It is dark brown on top and white with blackish streaks below.

**✳ OTHER FEATURES**
It has a long tail and broad, gray eyebrows.

**✳ BEHAVIOR**
When it flies, it pumps its tail up and down. Its call sounds like *tchimp*.

You can easily recognize a song sparrow by the dark patch on the center of its breast.

# DARK-EYED JUNCO

The dark-eyed junco (JUN-koe) usually lives in pine forests in the northern United States but is found in other areas during winter. It hops around on the ground, picking up insects, larvae, and seeds.

## WHERE TO FIND:
Dark-eyed juncos live in pine forests and woods. In winter, you often see them at bird feeders.

## WHAT TO LOOK FOR:

**✳ SIZE**
A dark-eyed junco is about six inches long.

**✳ COLOR**
It is smooth and gray on the back, white underneath, and has a black or gray hood.

**✳ OTHER FEATURES**
It has a pink bill and dark eyes.

**✳ BEHAVIOR**
It flicks its tail while it flies and when it searches for food.

You can tell from its gray side feathers that this dark-eyed junco is from eastern North America.

FIELD NOTES

In the East this bird is gray. In the West, it has a brown back and pink sides. In the Midwest it has white wingbars.

Midwestern

Eastern

Western

# BOBOLINK

 The male bobolink (BOB-uh-link) has a loud, bubbling song that sounds like *bob-o-link, bob-o-link*. Bobolinks gather in large flocks during fall before migrating to South America.

## WHERE TO FIND:
In summer look for bobolinks in hayfields, weedy meadows, and salt marshes.

## WHAT TO LOOK FOR:

✳ **SIZE**
Bobolinks are seven inches long—about as long as a pencil.

✳ **COLOR**
In spring, the male is black with a white rump. The back of the male's neck is tan. The female is pale brown.

✳ **OTHER FEATURES**
It has spiked tail feathers.

✳ **BEHAVIOR**
In summer it feeds on insects. In winter it eats mostly seeds.

Male bobolinks often sing only in flight. The females do not sing.

FIELD NOTES
After spring, male bobolinks shed their rich breeding plumage and become a pale brownish color.

# WESTERN MEADOWLARK

The western meadowlark has long legs and a long, pointed bill. Its speckled back feathers make it hard to see as it searches among grass clumps for insects and seeds. It is the state bird of Kansas, Montana, Nebraska, North Dakota, Oregon, and Wyoming.

Eastern meadowlark

## FIELD NOTES

Eastern and western meadowlarks look almost the same, but they sing different songs.

## WHERE TO FIND:

Western meadowlarks live around prairies and other areas of open country. They are usually on the ground.

## WHAT TO LOOK FOR:

**✳ SIZE**
A western meadowlark is just over nine inches long.

**✳ COLOR**
It is speckled brown on the back, and has a bright yellow breast with a black V on it.

**✳ OTHER FEATURES**
It has white outer tail feathers.

**✳ BEHAVIOR**
These birds live in pairs during summer. In winter, they form flocks.

The western meadowlark occasionally eats berries if insects or seeds are scarce.

# COMMON GRACKLE

 Common grackles usually live near farmland. They move around in large flocks, feeding mainly on worms. They also catch frogs and small fish near the edges of ponds and marshes.

## WHERE TO FIND:

You can see common grackles on farms, in city parks and gardens, and on suburban streets.

## WHAT TO LOOK FOR:

**✳ SIZE**

A common grackle is about 12 inches long—as long as an average ruler.

**✳ COLOR**

The male is black with a bronze or purplish sheen. The female is duller.

**✳ OTHER FEATURES**

It has a long, slender tail that is wide at the tip.

**✳ BEHAVIOR**

Its call is like the sound of a rusty gate swinging back and forth.

The common grackle has pale yellow eyes and a thick, curved bill.

FIELD NOTES

At dusk, flocks of grackles often gather to roost in shade trees along suburban streets.

# NORTHERN ORIOLE

 The northern oriole (OR-ee-OHL) is the state bird of Maryland. It spends the winter in Central America and returns to North America during May. It feeds mainly on insects.

## WHERE TO FIND:
Northern orioles live in the treetops in forests, and also in parks and gardens.

## WHAT TO LOOK FOR:

✴ **SIZE**
Northern orioles are about seven inches long—as long as a pencil.

✴ **COLOR**
Males are bright orange and black. Females have greenish plumage with dull orange breasts.

✴ **OTHER FEATURES**
They have rich, flutelike songs.

✴ **BEHAVIOR**
In winter, northern orioles often visit bird feeders.

The oriole's nest is built like a hammock high in a tree fork. It swings in the wind so that the chicks do not fall out.

FIELD NOTES

In western North America, the male oriole's face is orange. In eastern states, its head is jet black.

Western oriole

# PURPLE FINCH

 Large, twittering flocks of purple finches feed on seeds, flower buds, and plant shoots high in the treetops. The purple finch is the state bird of New Hampshire. It has a *tik* or *tuk* call.

## WHERE TO FIND:

In summer, purple finches live in pine trees. In winter, they prefer thickets and shrubbery.

## WHAT TO LOOK FOR:

**✳ SIZE**
A purple finch is almost as long as this book.

**✳ COLOR**
The male is brownish, with a red head, breast, and rump. The female is brown.

**✳ OTHER FEATURES**
It has a sharp, cone-shaped bill.

**✳ BEHAVIOR**
The purple finch's long, rambling warble is more melodious than the song of any other finch.

The purple finch has a long, rambling, warbling song.

FIELD NOTES

Purple finches do not migrate in winter because they eat seeds that are available all year.

Female

# WHITE-WINGED CROSSBILL

The white-winged crossbill nests in pine forests across Canada. It visits the northern United States only in winter. It is an active and tame bird. It has a long, sweet, canary-like song.

**FIELD NOTES**

Crossbills pry open spruce and pine cones with their bills to eat the seeds inside.

## WHERE TO FIND:
You'll find these birds in fields, gardens, and parks, where they eat insects and seeds from weeds.

## WHAT TO LOOK FOR:

**\* SIZE**
A white-winged crossbill is about six inches long.

**\* COLOR**
The male is dull red with black wings and tail. The female is dull brown with a yellow rump.

**\* OTHER FEATURES**
The male has bold white wing bars.

**\* BEHAVIOR**
In harsh winters, it sometimes travels much farther south than usual.

The white-winged crossbill's call is a sharp *cheet* sound.

# AMERICAN GOLDFINCH

 The American goldfinch is the state bird of Iowa, New Jersey, and Washington. In its summer plumage, the male is one of North America's most colorful birds.

## WHERE TO FIND:
You may see these birds feeding among roadside weeds, and in parks and overgrown gardens.

## WHAT TO LOOK FOR:

**✴ SIZE**
American goldfinches are about five inches long.

**✴ COLOR**
The male is brilliant yellow, with black wings, cap, and tail. The female is brown, with black wings and tail.

**✴ OTHER FEATURES**
In winter, the male is brown.

**✴ BEHAVIOR**
It builds its nest very late in summer and lines it with thistle seeds.

The American goldfinch has a trilling, rambling song. It often mimics the songs of other birds.

FIELD NOTES

American goldfinches harvest the unripe seeds of thistles before they fall to the ground.

# GLOSSARY

**Bill** The beak, or jaws, of a bird.

**Breed** When adult males and females come together to produce young.

**Call** A sound a bird makes.

**Crest** The feathers that stand up on the top of a bird's head.

**Crown** The top of a bird's head.

**Eave** The part of the roof that hangs over the walls of a building.

**Forage** To search or hunt for food.

**Larvae** An insect's wormlike stage when it is between the egg and adult stages.

**Melodious** To have a tune. Pleasant to listen to.

**Migrate** To travel to another area to find food or to breed.

**Mimic** To copy. Some birds often copy sounds made by other birds.

**Perch** A branch or other place where a bird rests or sleeps.

**Plumage** The feathers that cover a bird's body.

**Prairie**  A huge area of grassland.

**Prey**  Any creature hunted by other creatures for food.

**Pry**  To force something open.

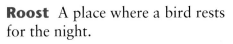

**Roost**  A place where a bird rests for the night.

**Rump**  An area on a bird's back just above the base of its tail.

**Salt marsh**  A damp, swampy area that is often covered with seawater.

**Sheen**  The shine on the surface of something.

**Song**  A special kind of call a bird makes to attract a mate or protect its territory.

**Thicket**  A thick growth of bushes or small trees.

**Trill**  The sound when two or more notes are repeated very quickly, one after the other.

**Undergrowth/Underbrush**  Small trees or bushes growing underneath larger trees.

**Wingbars**  The large stripes that run across the wings of some birds.

# INDEX OF
# **GARDEN BIRDS**

**Bluebird 30**
**Bobolink 62**
**Bunting 56**
**Bushtit 20**
**Cardinal 52**
**Chickadee 18**
**Crossbill 72**
**Crow 16**
**Dipper 26**
**Finch 70**
**Flycatcher 10**
**Goldfinch 74**
**Grackle 66**

Hummingbird 6
Jay 14
Junco 60
Kinglet 28
Meadowlark 64
Mockingbird 36
Nuthatch 22
Oriole 68
Robin 34
Shrike 42
Sparrow 58
Starling 44
Swallow 12
Thrasher 38
Thrush 32
Towhee 54
Vireo 46
Warbler 48
Waxwing 40
Woodpecker 8
Wren 24
Yellowthroat 50

# PHOTOGRAPHIC CREDITS

**front cover** Wayne Cankinen/Bruce Coleman Ltd. **back cover** Larry West/FLPA **half title page** S. Maslowski/FLPA **title page** Marie Read/Bruce Coleman Ltd. **4** Marie Read/Bruce Coleman Ltd. **5** Robert A. Tyrell/Oxford Scientific Films **7** Wayne Lankinen/Bruce Coleman Ltd. **9** Leonard Lee Rue III/Bruce Coleman Ltd. **11** Bates Littlehales/NGS Image Collection **13** Roger Tidman/NHPA **15** John Snyder/Planet Earth Pictures **17** Martin B. Withers/FLPA **19** Wayne Lankinen/Bruce Coleman Ltd. **21** P. La Tourette/ VIREO **23** Marie Read/Bruce Coleman Ltd. **25** S. Maslowski/FLPA **27** Dieter & Mary Plage/Bruce Coleman Ltd. **29** Johann Schumacher/VIREO **31** Wayne Lankinen/ Bruce Coleman Ltd. **33** L. West/FLPA **35** Robert Erwin/NHPA**37** John Shaw/NHPA **39** S. Maslowski/FLPA **41** Wayne Lankinen/ Bruce Coleman Ltd. **43** A. R. Hamblin/FLPA **45** Susan & Allen Parker/ARPS/Planet Earth Pictures **47** A. Morris/VIREO **49** Bates Littlehales/NGS Image Collection **51** Roger Tidman/FLPA **53** Tom Ulrich/Oxford Scientific Films **55** Brian Kenney/Planet Earth Pictures **57** Tom Ulrich/Oxford Scientific Films **59** Frank Schneidermeyer/ Oxford Scientific Films **61** Wayne Lankinen/Bruce Coleman Ltd. **63** Marie Read/Bruce Coleman Ltd. **65** Michael Gore/FLPA **67** Robert P. Carr/Bruce Coleman Ltd. **69** Dr. Scott Nielson/Bruce Coleman Ltd. **71** Wayne Lankinen/Bruce Coleman Ltd. **73** B. Henry/VIREO **75** Wayne Lankinen/Bruce Coleman Ltd. **76** Gordon Langsbury/Bruce Coleman Ltd. **77** Stephen J. Krasemann/Bruce Coleman Ltd. **78 (top)** Larry West/FLPA **78 (bottom)** Kim Taylor/Bruce Coleman Ltd. **79** Richard Day/Oxford Scientific Films

The world's largest nonprofit scientific and educational organization, the National Geographic Society was founded in 1888 "for the increase and diffusion of geographic knowledge." Since then it has supported scientific exploration and spread information to its more than eight million members worldwide.

The National Geographic Society educates and inspires millions every day through magazines, books, television programs, videos, maps and atlases, research grants, the National Geographic Bee, teacher workshops, and innovative classroom materials.

The Society is supported through membership dues, charitable gifts, and income from the sale of its educational products.

Members receive NATIONAL GEOGRAPHIC magazine—the Society's official journal—discounts on Society products, and other benefits.

For more information about the National Geographic Society, its educational programs, publications, or ways to support its work, please call 1-800-NGS-LINE (647-5463), or write to the following address:

National Geographic Society
1145 17th Street, N.W.
Washington, D.C. 20036-4688 U.S.A.

Visit the Society's Web site:
www.nationalgeographic.com

# FIELD NOTES

# FIELD NOTES

# SKETCHES

# FIELD NOTES

# SKETCHES

# FIELD NOTES

# SKETCHES

# FIELD NOTES

# SKETCHES

# FIELD NOTES

# SKETCHES

# FIELD NOTES

# SKETCHES

# FIELD NOTES